Classic Coasters

A celebration of short-sea shipping

Paul Boot and Roy Fenton

Photographs also from Malcolm Donnelly, Eddie Jackson, Stan Tedford, Jim McFaul, Len Bath, Nigel Bowker, John Clarkson, Harold Appleyard, H. Christiansen, Les Hodder, Nigel Jones, Michael J. Krieger, John Slavin, John Wiltshire, and the World Ship Photo Library.

Ships in Focus Publications in conjunction with

PRIAM
PUBLICATIONS

Published in the UK in 1997 by Ships in Focus Publications,
18 Franklands, Longton
Preston PR4 5PD

ISBN 0 9521179 8 3

Reproduction and Printing by Amadeus Press Ltd., Huddersfield.

s page

set for the classic steam coaster, an obedient servant of industry and commerce for a hundred years. Dressed overall, the **Craigolive** *(605g/1920) sails from Donegall y, Belfast for the last time on 31st March 1965, heading for Passage West, Cork and shipbreakers. The Barnstaple-built coaster had completed 35 years service on the Sea for Belfast owners Hugh Craig and Co. Ltd.*
Stan Tedford

INTRODUCTION

The authors cheerfully confess to having selected for their title two words which are easier to understand than to define. 'Classic' we have chosen to interpret as 'belonging to a bygone period which is remembered with affection' - namely the 1950s and 1960s when we first took an interest in ships. These decades saw the happy conjunction of the survival of many older ships with the availability of good colour film. Hence, with the unstinting help of a number of photographers active then, we have been able to present this celebration of pre- and post-war steamers and motorships which look to us how small ships ought to look.

Allowing only a strict definition of the word 'coasters' would preclude many small ships on the grounds that they made short sea voyages. It would also include many large tankers and bulk carriers which were capable of crossing oceans but whose owners chose to employ them on coastal passages. Instead, we have fallen back on the accepted understanding of a coaster as a ship small enough to enter a wide variety of ports and harbours, but capable of comfortably crossing unsheltered waters such as the Irish, North and Baltic Seas, and even trading to the Mediterranean. Thus we have included vessels ranging in size from Clyde puffers, through coastal colliers to steamers whose regular trade took them to the Baltic, White Sea and Mediterranean.

The captions explore why the ships in the photos look the way they do, but it is worth considering why today's coasters are so much less attractive. The container is one of the causes; the requirement to stow boxes as easily as possible meaning that decks are dead flat and sheer is invariably absent. Superstructure has grown narrower and taller to maximise deck space. No self-respecting port can now survive without its own craneage, so not even bulk-carrying coasters require cargo gear. Perhaps the worst factor has been the lemming-like rush to join the low air-draft club. True, trade has expanded at inland ports where access is restricted by low bridges, but not to anything like the extent of the increase in numbers of ships able to squeeze under these bridges. As a result, many of today's coasters have all the aesthetic appeal of a plank.

What remains of the classic coaster today? Almost all have gone from mainstream European trades, although a few small and satisfyingly old motor coasters can still be seen put-putting through the Kiel Canal to small ports on the Elbe and Baltic. At the far end of the Mediterranean, a dwindling band of superannuated hulls rust on under the Greek and Turkish flags. The Caribbean is now almost the last refuge of the old motorship which is too small to be economic on the coast of Europe. Sadly, one can look almost in vain for such ships in museums. Britain's **Robin** is an absolute gem, probably unique in the world as an example of a steam-driven, pure cargo ship from the nineteenth century, but she has been shockingly neglected of late. The Dutch have a few motor coasters in various states of preservation and the Swedes one. But it is likely that for future generations it will be easier to find an example of a wooden sailing vessel than one of the steam or diesel coasters which replaced it, and which played such a major part in building Europe's industry and trade.

In writing the captions we have mused on aspects of the ship's design, the history of its trade, the fortunes of the owner, or the coaster's career where this was significant. In other words, we have pointed out whatever we think is interesting. Our two rules have been to mention every previous or subsequent name, and to give an indication of what finally happened to the ship, unless it is one of the few which is known to survive - histories having been checked to August 1997. Our initial resolve to put the ships in a strictly chronological order of building weakened as we came to appreciate the advantages of grouping ships of one type, trade or owner together, and of achieving variety in the sequence of locations. A very rough chronology has been maintained, but Clyde puffers, colliers, the few tankers, and some other groups have been kept together.

Lastly, it is our pleasant task to thank all those who made this book possible: the photographers who generously loaned us their priceless transparencies; those who helped with researching the captions and especially Anne Cowne of *Lloyd's Register*, David Burrell and Ken Garrett; plus Richard Cook, David Crossland and their colleagues at Amadeus Press, and Angela Swaine at Highlight Type Bureau.

Paul Boot,   Roy Fenton,
Barnston   Wimbledon
                                                                                              September 1997

Front cover:
Same again, please: a second round of **Guinness.** *Making a speedy return after her appearance in Priam Publications's A River in Retrospect,* **Guinness** *(1,151g/1931) is perfectly reflected in the still waters of the Manchester Ship Canal near Warrington. Spared the rough and tumble of the coastal bulk trades, few fleets were so impeccably maintained as that of Arthur Guinness, Son and Co. (Dublin) Ltd. Although displaced as the company's flagship in 1952 (see page 48),* **Guinness** *was not withdrawn from her Dublin to Manchester service for another eleven years.*   Eddie Jackson

Back cover:
Here in August 1963 is one of the very last single-hatch, coal-fired steam coasters in its natural environment: a small Irish Sea harbour. Ports like Douglas on the Isle of Man were limited, not only in the size of their berths, but also in the consignments of cargo they could accept. So smaller coasters like **Conister** *(411g/1921) survived in the Irish Sea trades, long after they were uneconomic elsewhere. The Isle of Man Steam Packet Co. Ltd. - better known for its more glamorous passenger steamers - owned* **Conister** *from 1932 until 1965 when she was towed away from Douglas to be broken up on the Clyde.*   H. Christiansen

AKSEL 1   1913   497g   Gazanfer Akar, Istanbul

There can be no denying that **Aksel 1** is both a classic and a coaster. She was a typical raised-quarter deck vessel, of a type refined and built by the hundreds in British yards. In her case builders were R. Williamson and Son of Workington, who turned to coastal ships as the market for large steel sailing ships declined in the 1890s. As a coaster the credentials of **Aksel 1** are impeccable, she being originally the steamer **Volana** of a Liverpool company engaged in regular cargo services on the West Coast of the UK. **Volana** and her owners became part of the mighty Coast Lines group in 1919, the name **Cornish Coast** being adopted in the interests of corporate identity. In 1935 she began to move down the social scale, so to speak, becoming the coastal tramp **Kyle Queen**, and in 1951 passed to a sequence of Turkish owners, who renamed her **Kardesler, Meso, Emel,** and finally **Aksel 1**. In 1961 she was rebuilt at Istanbul, gaining an Italian diesel engine but losing her steamer's elegant funnel, her steam steering gear and steam winches, although she retained much of her classic lines. When photographed she was tramping out of Istanbul to the Black Sea ports and south to Izmir, a service in which she received as many hard knocks as in her early years on the British coast. Proof of her powers of endurance, however, is that she is still afloat in 1997, after 84 remarkable years.

Michael J. Krieger, Bosphorus, October 1982

3

ÄOLUS 1908 941g Captain Herbert Wietzke, Holtenau

As explained in the introduction, the compilers have been unable to resist including several examples of classic Baltic-type steamers which were a much-loved part of the short-sea shipping scene right up to the 1960s.

Äolus was built by Burmeister & Wain in Copenhagen for local owners as **Washington** *but soon became the Danish* **Lilleborg** *and then the German* **Adrana.** *She had the misfortune to be in Rouen on the outbreak of war in August 1914, and the French Navy took her over, initially as the transport* **Marguerite.** *Later, as a Q-ship, she tried her best to*

lure unsuspecting U-boat commanders within range of her hidden guns. In 1923 she returned to Scandinavia as the Swedish **Helle,** *a name she retained until 1959 when Finns bought her and renamed her* **Markus.** *She had become German again not long before being photographed, and as* **Äolus** *survived until May 1964 when sold to shipbreakers in her native Denmark.*

Malcolm Donnelly, Dunston Staithes, River Tyne, 12th September 1962

SPARTAK   1909   2,105g   Sovtorgflot, Leningrad

Sometimes echoes of long-ago events come down to us over the years. Crossing the Baltic on 24th October 1915 was the German steamer **Gerda Vith,** *recently bought from other German owners who had her built as* **Margarete Gelpcke.** *She had the misfortune to fall in with the Russian submarine* **Alligator** *which was, of course, an Imperial Russian submarine. At a time when war was still being waged in a gentlemanly fashion, the steamer was captured and entered the service of the Tsar's navy as a transport known simply as* **U.** *Following the 1917 revolution she was one of the first ships to come under the control of the Bolshevik government and, looking for an appropriately revolutionary name, they chose* **Spartak.** *Hence, captured on Kodachrome in an English river in 1964, we have a reminder*

not only of the events of October 1917 that changed the history of the world, but also of an earlier but unsuccessful communist revolution in Germany, that of the Spartacists. **Spartak** *has clearly been rebuilt at some time, probably as a result of damage in the Second World War. She was broken up in 1969, two years after having been removed from the USSR registry following the arrival of a new* **Spartak** *from a Hungarian yard. An opportunity had been missed to build her replacement in the same yard, A.G. Neptun of Rostock, which was then in East Germany and building ships for the USSR.*

Malcolm Donnelly, Dunston Staithes, River Tyne, 2nd May 1964

5

SAN PAWL   1920   1,591gt   Jakobson (Malta) Ltd., Valletta

Swedish shipping and shipbuilding grew rapidly in the early years of the twentieth century, after a period when both were very much eclipsed by those of Britain. Although Swedish ships faced many difficulties during the First World War - North Sea minefields being no respecters of neutrality - the shipping industry did very well, thank you. High quality iron ore was shipped from the Gulf of Bothnia to Germany, whilst across the North Sea there was an equally lucrative traffic with the UK. As a result, there was money to spend on ships when peace came, and the Swedish shipbuilding industry was in a position to supply the demand. Typical of ships built mainly for the short-sea trades was **Burgundia**, *completed at Malmo: note the generous amount of woodwork around the wheelhouse.*

Burgundia *would spend most of her life carrying timber out of the Baltic, probably returning with coal or coke from a British, Dutch or Belgian port. Unusually, she spent over 40 years doing this under the same name. In 1961 she was renamed* **San Pawl** *and although her owners sound Swedish, she was registered in Malta, which at that time meant she flew the red ensign. Under her final name,* **Robertina,** *and now with definite Maltese owners, she put into Kristiansand with engine trouble on 17th August 1967. This proved fatal, as she was never repaired but towed to Grimstad and there broken up.*

Malcolm Donnelly, Dunston Staithes, River Tyne, 22nd June 1962

6

MARVEL 1921 1,595g Hartwig Larsen, Haugesund

If further excuse is needed for the presence of Baltic-type steamers like **Marvel** *in a book entitled* Classic Coasters *it can be argued that such engines-amidships vessels were long a common sight on the British coast and especially on the Tyne, with many coastal collier owners preferring this type to the engines-aft design. Putting the machinery amidships helped to better distribute stresses on the hull, but meant a shaft tunnel which reduced carrying capacity in the after hold.*

Marvel *was built for local owners by Akers M/V at what was then Christiania but soon became Oslo. In 1951 she was bought by Hartwig Larsen of Haugesund who had just lost his only ship, the* **Sado,** *which capsized and sank in the Baltic during the previous November. Larsen kept* **Marvel** *until 1967 when she was sold and renamed* **Johs Stove**.

Renaming a ship was once considered an unlucky action, and it proved unfortunate for this vessel which, after an uneventful 46 years under one name, never traded again. She remained laid up at Haugesund until towed away to Grimstad where she arrived in September 1968 to be broken up.

The **Marvel** *appears to be entering the Tyne in ballast, with no sign of the timber deck cargo that the upright supports would suggest. She must be arriving to load coke, a light cargo which would fill her holds before she was down to her marks. A deck cargo would then be loaded, kept in place by wire mesh attached to the uprights.*

Malcolm Donnelly, North Shields, 1963

TYNE   1920   1,168 g   Compania Maritima Tees S.A., Panama (Arthur Jurgenthal, Stockholm)

Scandinavian steam shipowners often began by purchasing old British tonnage, but by the 1920s local shipbuilding industries had developed to the extent that they could meet local needs. Indeed, a Norwegian yard produced its own design for local requirements, the Fredrikstad type. Although built at Skien in Norway, the **Tyne** *is otherwise a good example of this design. Her hull has a forecastle, bridge deck and poop, with distinct wells between the islands. Masts or kingposts are positioned at the ends of the wells to give the maximum*

clear space to stow a deck cargo of timber or coke.

Before becoming **Tyne** *in 1958 she had already carried the names* **Grete, Dalheim** *and* **Ligur.** *Lying in the eponymous river, the* **Tyne** *had just over a year of further work to do before arriving at Lübeck in September 1963 to be broken up.*

Malcolm Donnelly, Dunston Staithes, River Tyne, 10th August 1962

HINRICH PETERS   1925   1,234g   H. Peters, Hamburg

German shipowners did not generally adopt the classic raised-quarter deck, engines-aft British coaster, preferring the larger engines-amidships design. As **Hinrich Peters** shows here, this design was widely used for carrying timber from the Baltic. This being the Tyne, the cargo may well be pit props. **Hinrich Peters** was not built for German owners, but for a shipowner who today has one of the world's largest fleets, A.P. Moller of Copenhagen. As **Effie Maersk** the ship came from Moller's own yard, Odense Staalskibs, which today builds some of the world's largest container ships.

When Moller finished with the ship in 1954 she ran as **Rombus,** registered in Costa Rica. Renamed **Hinrich Peters** in 1956, the ageing steamer then played a part in the rebirth of the German merchant fleet. This had been almost completely annihilated, not just by bombing and torpedoing, which had left most of the fleet disabled, but by the reparations exacted by the Allies. Once the occupying powers allowed German owners to begin acquiring ships again, straitened economic circumstances meant they could buy only well-used tonnage. At the time it was difficult to foresee that the German coastal fleet would rise from the ashes to become the most modern and largest in Western Europe. **Hinrich Peters** saw the beginning of this trend, and by the time it arrived at Hamburg to be broken up in 1963 its home port was already alive with modern, German-built and owned motor coasters.   *Malcolm Donnelly, North Shields, 13th September 1963*

LOCH LINNHE   1928   766g   V. Nolan Ltd., Dublin

Loch Linnhe *illustrates how the steam coaster remained a good servant of industry until the very end. A classic British design from a Goole yard, she was nevertheless built for owners in Antwerp who named her* **Anna**. *The owner's satisfaction with her is apparent from their retaining* **Anna** *until 1955, when she found a Northern Irish buyer, although she was registered in Glasgow and later Dublin as* **Loch Linnhe**. *It was under this name that the ageing steamer found herself part of the unit load revolution during the mid-1960s, operating between Preston and the port of Greenore. As can be seen, her deck cargo consisted largely of laden trailers which, although needing lifting off with cranes, could then be conveyed to their destination by road without further ado. Like so many cargo ships engaged on unit load trades,* **Loch Linnhe** *has lost her derricks, but she has gained a radar set. During 1965 she was replaced on this route by a new motor vessel, but her owner then transferred her to a service between Wicklow and Rotterdam or Antwerp. She was now on charter to George Bell & Co., a company which came to dominate the container trade between Ireland and Continental Europe until its recent financial troubles.* **Loch Linnhe** *herself arrived in tow at Troon to be broken up by the West of Scotland Shipbreaking Co. Ltd. on the very first day of 1966.*

John Clarkson, River Ribble

CRAIGANTLET 1931 827g Hugh Craig and Co. Ltd., Belfast

Craigantlet *is a fine example of the classic British steam coaster, still coal-fired, still with a full cargo gear, and still hauling bulk cargoes - mainly but not exclusively coal - until the mid-1960s. She was built rather late, as by 1931 the diesel engine had proved its virtues, but there is an interesting story to* **Craigantlet's** *origins. As a speculation Glasgow owner John Stewart and Co. bought some war-surplus tug engines, but could not find buyers. Already the owner of one or two coasters, Stewart approached Scott and Sons of Bowling and asked them to build six coaster hulls to take the steam engines. One of the results was* **Yewarch***, which traded for Stewart and his successors mainly on the East Coast of the UK,*

carrying coal south and cement north. In 1957 she passed to long-established Belfast owners Hugh Craig and Co. who renamed her **Craigantlet***. Her trading was now largely confined to the Irish Sea, still usually with coal from ports such as Preston, a cargo she is probably about to load as she steams up the Ribble in this photograph. Occasionally she also helped out on Craig's general cargo service between Preston and Belfast. By 1965 even owners such as Craig who had clung to steam in the short-distance Irish Sea trades had to admit that it had outlived its usefulness, and in September* **Craigantlet** *made her way to Passage West, County Cork to be broken up.* John Clarkson, River Ribble

BALLYKESH   1935   869g   John Kelly Ltd., Belfast

*The difference between a coaster and a collier was often one of employment rather than design. In their heyday, steam coasters may well have spent a large proportion of their time shifting coal - so important was it in the coastal trade - but would be able to carry stone, ore, grain or other bulk cargoes if conditions or ownership changed. **Ballykesh** was virtually indistinguishable from steam coasters such as **Craigantlet**, but with her owners being major Northern Ireland coal merchants, she was exclusively engaged in carrying coal and can thus be regarded as a collier.*

In the East Coast coal trade, specialist colliers did evolve as exemplified by ships featured later in this book. But owners on the Irish Sea remained rather conservative, and stayed

with established and successful designs. Thus in the 1930s we find Kellys ordering no fewer than eight traditional ships from John Lewis and Sons Ltd. of Aberdeen who also built their coal-burning steam engines. One of the few concessions to progress can be seen in this view, a cruiser stern rather than a counter.

***Ballykesh** had been **Baronscourt** until 1952, the renaming of the fleet following a change in ownership of Kellys, who were acquired jointly by Powell Duffryn Ltd. and William Cory and Son Ltd. Despite her obsolescence, **Ballykesh** steamed on until May 1964, when she left Swansea - a familiar haunt for a coal boat - for Antwerp and the breakers.*

Jim McFaul, Preston, 7th April 1963

THE PRESIDENT   1936   926g   John Hay and Sons Ltd., Glasgow

*With her counter stern, **The President** is a more traditional design than **Ballykesh**, although she has no mizzen mast. The latter was an anachronistic feature, dating from the earlier part of the twentieth century when most steam coasters would carry - and use - a suit of sails. By the 1930s the mizzen was redundant, and in some coasters it was removed during the Second World War as it restricted the arc of fire when anti-aircraft guns were fitted on the poop.*

***The President** is a further example of the coaster/collier dilemma. Her owners were in home trade tramping, but their ships had grown so big that they were employed mainly in the East Coast coal trade. Her cargo gear and ownership made **The President** a coaster,*

but her regular employment classified her as a collier.

*The Hay family were deeply involved with the stories of both the diminutive Clyde puffer, and the larger steam coaster. Beginning in business at Kirkintilloch on the Forth and Clyde Canal in 1867, they initially built and operated the steam lighters which grew to become puffers. In 1890, John Hay had a coaster called **The Prince** built, and developed this business alongside the puffer fleet. Hay's coasters steadily grew in size, so that **The President** measured over 200 feet in length. Built at Troon, she returned there some 26 years later to be broken up. By then, John Hay's coaster business had been sold to F.T. Everard and Sons Ltd.   Malcolm Donnelly, Pelaw Main, River Tyne, 1961*

13

ALEXANDRA K 1943 2,908g Compania Marabello San Nicolas, Panama (J.P. Katsoulakos and J.T.W. McTaggart, London)

The three-island, engines-amidships steamer became so closely associated with Swedish and Norwegian owners that when the British government decided to build to this design as part of their wartime programme, the name Scandinavian *was given to the type. Carrying timber from the Baltic was definitely not on the agenda in 1941 when the first,* **Empire Wolfe,** *was completed. The attraction of the well decks clear of cargo gear was the ability to load bulky deck cargoes, especially of tanks and other military vehicles, and the type was much used in convoys to North Russia.*

Alexandra K *was built as* **Empire Valour** *by William Gray & Co. Ltd. of West Hartlepool, a yard which had a prodigious output of fairly plain cargo ships, including many for Scandinavian owners. After the war she found British owners as* **Eskgarth** *and later*

Uskmouth *and would trade largely to the Mediterranean, although making occasional voyages to Canada and the Baltic for timber. As* **Uskmouth** *she frequently carried cargoes of esparto grass from North Africa. Her unencumbered decks were particularly suitable for this bulky but light material, delivered to Scottish East Coast ports for paper making, and after unloading* **Uskmouth** *would carry Tyne coal to Spain. She became* **Alexandra K** *in 1963, continuing to load coal at Newcastle, and retaining her wartime rig of high radio mast but no topmasts. Five years later further Greek owners renamed her* **Aristiois II,** *as which she was broken up at Piraeus in 1971.*

Malcolm Donnelly, Dunston Staithes, River Tyne, 10th March 1963

LADY SHARON   1933   1,511g   Thomas Watson (Shipping) Ltd., Rochester

London's Surrey Docks handled a great deal of the capital's timber imports. By their last days, however, the sight of a British ship such as **Lady Sharon** *unloading timber was unusual, whilst her light blue hull bordered on the eccentric.*

Previously, **Lady Sharon** *had just one careful owner: J. Lauritzen of Denmark. She had been built as* **Laura**, *a steamer but a sophisticated one.* **Laura** *had a four-cylinder compound engine, and rather than use the steam a third time in a further low-pressure cylinder, it was made to drive a turbine. As built she had cooling plant in her hold for carrying fruit. Her hull form is unusual, too: a very long bridge deck making for a short well forward, which has a walkway bridging it.*

Laura *was in Montevideo when Denmark was invaded by Germany in 1940. After being laid up for a few months she was taken over by Uruguay, although they soon passed her on to the USA who ran her as* **Rocha**. *She was restored to her owners at the end of 1945, and was subsequently renamed* **Laura Dan**.

The Rochester company in whose ownership she is seen renamed her **Lady Sharon** *in January 1960, but she remained under the British flag for only 18 months. Owners whose address was in Beirut took her next, and as* **Tico** *under the Panama flag she ended her days at a Dutch breaker's yard late in 1966.*

Len Bath, Surrey Commercial Docks, 1961

MELLITE 1886 90g Ross and Marshall Ltd., Greenock

The Clyde puffer followed a different route of development from the larger conventional steam coaster. It originated as an inland craft on the Forth and Clyde Canal, where an abundance of fresh water allowed its primitive steam engine to do without a condenser, hence it puffed like a railway locomotive. The operators quickly saw the usefulness of extending the puffers' voyages into the Firth of Clyde and beyond, but this necessitated more sophisticated engines, plus the need to conserve fresh water. The puffer no longer puffed, but retained the peculiar and inconvenient feature of a steering position behind the funnel, as **Mellite** exemplifies. Even when they became the workhorses of the Firth of Clyde and the Western Isles, the puffers were still restricted in length by the 68 foot locks on the Forth and Clyde Canal and the slightly less constricting Crinan Canal, which kept them under 80 feet. However, the diminutive size of their vessels did not inhibit the hardy puffer men, who would think little of crossing the Minch or even St. George's Channel. **Mellite** was built as the unpowered lighter **Salisbury**, and only in 1904 was she equipped with a modestly-powered steam engine. Her remarkable survival into the late 1960s gives testimony to the usefulness of the puffer, which was equally at home carrying coal to a beach in the Western Isles or tending buoys in the Firth of Clyde. **Mellite**'s career finally ended at a Dalmuir scrap yard in 1968.

Jim McFaul, Firth of Clyde, 7th June 1967

COLONSAY   1944   96g   Alexander McNeil, Greenock

*The handiness of Clyde puffers commended them to the Admiralty who used them extensively in the First World War to serve the warships stationed at Scapa Flow and other remote anchorages. In the Second World War, the Admiralty were equally unprepared for the needs of victualling its fleet, but actually built puffers for themselves. Their Lordships took as their model the last two puffers which emerged before the war, **Anzac** and **Lascar** built at Bowling for J. Hay & Sons Ltd. These 64 craft were the VICs, short for victualling inshore craft.*

Although naval bases continued to find VICs useful well after the war, a number were sold to civilian operators, and their availability meant few puffers were built in post-war years.

*VIC 84 was completed at Thorne on the Ouse in 1944, but was not sold by the Admiralty until 1962. She became **Colonsay** as a replacement for her owner's previous puffer of the same name, ex-**VIC 63**, which foundered in 1960. The second **Colonsay** was sold on in 1966, finding owners in Somerset, but evidence of further trading is scant although she remained on the British registry well into the 1990s.*

***Colonsay** was a steamer, but several VICs were built with diesel engines or later converted. One conversion, **Eilean Eisdeal** ex-**VIC 72**, continued in commercial service on the West Coast of Scotland until 1996, illustrating that even a tiny coaster could make a living where water connections were better than land ones.*   Malcolm Donnelly, Greenock, 1962

CONFID   1928   199g   W. Visser, Sliedrecht

One factor in the decline of the British coasting steamer between the wars was the apparently unstoppable rise of the Dutch motor coaster. During the First World War the diesel engine, previously regarded as interesting but unreliable, was developed to the extent that both British and German navies could trust it to take their submarines as far as the Eastern Mediterranean. No-one exploited the potential of this new technology better than the Dutch, whose fleet had profited from their neutrality by working for both sides during the conflict. In the depressed trading conditions of the 1920s and 1930s, tiny, grey-hulled motor coasters like this one made the most of the diesel's advantage of lower running costs, compactness and light weight. They could undercut British steamers and had the advantage of a shallow draft which increased their trading range.

*The longevity of **Confid**, which was sold to Belgian breakers only in 1973, owed much to the repairs carried out after she ran aground near Whitby in March 1955. By then she was named **Lea**, having previously been known as **Havik** and **Wea**. In dense fog **Lea** stranded at the foot of cliffs in such a position that even the renowned Dutch salvage experts had trouble getting her off, and had to resort to building a slipway. Abandoned to her underwriters, she was repaired in Rotterdam and as **Confid** went on to give her enterprising buyer a further 18 years of service.*

Paul Boot, Nieuwe Waterweg, 19th May 1972

MERSEY COAST 1938 509g Coast Lines Ltd., Liverpool

Through ambition and acquisition Coast Lines came to be the UK's largest operator of coasters. Ambition was supplied by Alfred Read, the architect of a strategy which saw three major coastal liner companies merge in 1913, and four years later adopt the title Coast Lines Ltd. Subsequent membership of Kylsant's Royal Mail Group provided the wherewithal in money and promises for Coast Lines to buy up a large slice of the British coastal liner business. Usually the businesses' owners, battered by losses during the First World War but flattered by excess profits, were only too glad to sell up and retire in comfort.

Coast Lines extracted themselves well from the Royal Mail Group's collapse in the 1930s, and positively benefited from Kylsant's championing of the motor vessel. Noting the

example of Dutch vessels like that opposite, Coast Lines built little other than motor coasters from the 1930s, and these ships served them well. **Mersey Coast** *was ordered from a yard in Alblasserdam, and ran for 30 years in Coast Lines' core fleet and that of subsidiary British Channel Islands Shipping Co. Ltd. When sold in 1967 she found the almost inevitable Greek owner, but came to a sad end when under the name of* **Agios Artemis** *she foundered in the Indian Ocean on the last day of May 1971.*

Mersey Coast's *deck cargo is worth examining: the two Bedford Dormobile vans have aircraft steps built on to them, presumably for use at Dublin Airport.*

Stan Tedford, Dublin, 1966

19

CAPETAN ANDREAS   1929   2,666g   Siconen Shipping S.A., Panama (Kyriakos B. Spiliopoulos, Athens)

*The involvement of William Cory and Sons in the coal trade goes back to 1785, long before the development of the steam collier. In 1861 the company introduced an impressive, if expensive, technological innovation by instituting floating derricks in the Thames. On a notoriously congested waterway this speeded the unloading of coal from sea-going ships into lighters and made it economic to build steam colliers, the first of which, the **Samuel Laing**, joined the fleet in the same year. It had been only ten years previously that the first efficient steam collier had been built, the **John Bowes**.*

*Corys later abandoned the naming of their colliers after worthies in the coal and gas industry and adopted names beginning with Cor. Most of their previous steamers had their machinery amidships, and **Corglen** was one of the first to have her engines aft with masts set between each pair of hatches. The design was already something of a classic, and, as subsequent pages show, it would see out the steam collier.*

*Sold in 1955 **Corglen** became **Michael A** and, from 1961, **Capetan Andreas**, as seen here. The latter's owning company had its brass plate in Panama but registered its ship in Liberia, presumably to make it as difficult as possible for taxman or creditor to interfere with its making a profit. In 1966 **Capetan Andreas** was sold to Spanish shipbreakers and arrived in tow at El Ferrol on 15th March.*

Malcolm Donnelly, Dunston Staithes, River Tyne, 2nd April 1963

20

CORMULL 1942 2,865g William Cory & Sons Ltd., London

During the Second World War merchant shipbuilding was given high priority from the outset - the importance of the merchant navy to an island nation being one lesson which was learned from the First World War, although it has subsequently been forgotten. Ships were built to standard designs, usually based on a recent successful vessel with the frills reduced to expedite production. During hostilities standard ships were completed for government account, and shipowners were granted licences to order ships for themselves only if they were to an existing design. William Cory & Sons Ltd. took advantage of this concession, its collier fleet having suffered heavily in the early years of the war when the East Coast route was subject to mines, E-boats and the Luftwaffe: all these dangers being endured to get coal to London. The steamer **Cormull** was built to the design of the company's **Cormarsh**, which was built in 1939 and torpedoed by an E-boat in November 1941. Note how since **Corglen** stems had become raked and derricks had been eliminated. **Cormull** was completed at Sunderland in July 1942, but only eight months later was badly damaged when she detonated a mine off Yarmouth. Repaired, she carried the name **Coldharbour** from 1946 to 1949 afterwards reverting to **Cormull**. When Corys sold her in 1960 she became the Greek-owned **Christakis** and sailed as this until November 1965, when a collision in the Dardanelles left her fit only for scrap.

Malcolm Donnelly, North Shields

PORTWOOD 1941 2,934g
Wm. France, Fenwick and Co. Ltd., London

*During the Second World War, gun turrets for the **King George V** battleships were often fabricated at some distance from the yard building the hulls, and were so unwieldy that they could only be transported by sea. Hence two ships were built with hatches especially large to accommodate such turrets, the **Sea Fisher** and **Sound Fisher**. When not so employed, they carried East Coast coal, and belonged to a concern jointly owned by Fishers of Barrow, who had expertise in heavy lifts, and France, Fenwick, a senior collier company. After the war the joint owning company was wound up and **Sound Fisher** passed to France, Fenwick and, after a spell as **Colnbrook**, became **Portwood**. In comparison with her wartime role, her further career was rather mundane. After over 20 years plodding up and down the East Coast with coal, she was sold and became the **Chrysanthi** in 1962, and was broken up in Denmark in 1967. The deckhouse aft is notable: it was built to house the army gunners who helped defend merchant ships during the war.*

*Malcolm Donnelly, Dunston Staithes, River Tyne,
4th March 1962*

TAYLAN KALKAVAN 1945 1,997g
Kalkavan Denizcilik ve Ticaret A.S., Istanbul

*After the Second World War Wm. France, Fenwick and Co. Ltd. found themselves with an unbalanced fleet, war losses having been heavy in their ships of around 2,700 tons deadweight which were most suitable for the coal trade to London. Although preferring to build to their own specification they took four colliers completed to a design of the Gas, Light and Coke Co. for the Ministry of War Transport, tempted by prices which were well below current building costs. **Braywood** had been built as **Empire Vauxhall** at Grangemouth, and in August 1946 cost £76,000 - £30,000 less than the owners had recently paid Austins of Sunderland for the similar-sized **Moorwood**. Much less impressed with the performance of the Empire colliers than their own ships, France, Fenwick sold them relatively early, the coal-burning **Braywood** going to Turkish owners who renamed her **Abdullah** in 1960. In 1976 she became **Taylan Kalkavan**, as seen here, and was scrapped at Aliaga, Turkey in 1982.*

Nigel Jones, Bosphorus, 18th April 1981

LEVENWOOD 1945 1,058g Constantine Shipping Co. Ltd., Middlesbrough

Despite her name **Levenwood** *has no ownership connection with the ships opposite. Her Tees-side owners were no strangers to the coal trade - what owner was, especially on the East Coast - but had feet in other camps. They had a significant deep-sea tramping fleet, and ran ships on the Canadian coast. Even on the British coast their trading patterns were different from those of the pure collier owners, whose ships would steam north in ballast just as soon as they were unloaded. Constantine's ships would often carry coal southbound and return with a cargo of cement from the Medway to the North East. The modicum of cargo gear on* **Levenwood** *demonstrates her suitability for other trades than coal. Like* **Taylan Kalkavan** *opposite,* **Levenwood** *had been built for the British government*

during the Second World War. Her design was modelled on a ship called **Tudor Queen** *intended to carry coal from the East Coast to the Channel Isles. For a year after being built* **Levenwood** *had carried the name* **Empire Bromley** *whilst in the ownership of the Ministry of War Transport. When Constantine sold her in 1961, the steamer went to London owners whose sympathies were with Essex, and she was renamed* **Basildon**, *when reverting to the Kentish name Bromley would have had a certain satisfying symmetry.* **Basildon** *saw out her days under the Red Ensign, and was broken up in Belgium in 1967.*

Malcolm Donnelly, St. Peters, River Tyne, 31st May 1961

BRIMSDOWN 1951 1,837g Central Electricity Generating Board, London

The up-river collier, or 'flat-iron' as it became generally known, evolved because of the need to deliver extensive quantities of coal to London gas works. These works were sited above bridges which allowed nothing higher than a lighter to pass beneath. As early as 1878 colliers were specially built for this trade, of which the steamer **Brimsdown** *was a direct descendant. The bridge and accommodation were built as low as possible consistent with some degree of visibilty, whilst masts and funnels folded, or in later ships were telescopic. At 270 feet overall,* **Brimsdown** *was no tiddler, and navigating a vessel of this size on the tideway was a very skilled exercise. Not only had the master to ensure there was enough water under the keel when laden, but also enough air above the deck to clear the bridges*

when returning unladen. Only on a very few occasions did a 'flat-iron' lodge itself under a bridge, an event which would do little for the health of either.

Brimsdown *was one of the four last up-river steam colliers built, the choice of machinery being somewhat surprising as her owners - the nationalised electricity industry - had just taken delivery of two diesel-driven colliers of identical dimensions. Hardly surprisingly, the motor colliers outlasted the steamers, and* **Brimsdown** *was broken up on the Thames at Grays, Essex in October 1972. As a class, however, the up-river collier continued in service until 1980 when Battersea Power Station closed.*

Malcolm Donnelly, South Shields, 3rd June 1963

MENDIP 1950 1,362g
Central Electricity Generating Board, London.

The ending of the Second World War saw a massive expansion of electricity generation, and with it a great increase in the number of ships to carry the necessary fuel. With coal in abundance, and the mining and electricity industries being nationalised, it was unthinkable for power to be generated from imported oil.

Amongst the first ordered were ten steamers to carry coal to power stations in the south and south west of England, like that at Portsmouth where **Mendip** *has just unloaded. Above* **Mendip**'s *bridge is the number used to identify colliers when entering the Thames. The photograph also shows a Tiger class cruiser in the background.*

By no means did the state get full value out of this group of colliers. The anachronism of their steam engines and the electricity industry's abandonment of coal saw the smaller ones go early. **Mendip** *was sold in 1966, but Italians found her hull worthy of investment, converting her to a motor tanker. As* **Castelrosso** *and later just* **Rosso** *she lasted until 1994 when broken up in India.*

World Ship Photo Library, Camber Quay, Portsmouth, October 1963

JAMES ROWAN 1955 2,947g
Central Electricity Generating Board, London.

The electricity industry's - and indeed Britain's - last coastal steamers were a group of five colliers completed in 1954 and 1955. Oil burners with a big coal capacity, they were retained to serve power stations on the Thames, and all had respectable careers. The very last of the many hundreds of steam colliers built over a century was the **Sir Johnstone Wright** *of this class, completed in November 1955. The last in service, however, was* **James Rowan**. *Indeed, if an imaginative scheme to preserve her and use her hold as a local amenity had succeeded, she would have made a fitting memorial to the generations of colliers and their crews who helped heat and light London. But a rise in scrap prices meant her nationalised owners, bidden by their political masters to put cash above sentiment, sold her to breakers for more than the preservation trust could raise. On 6th June 1984 her arrival at Queenborough in Kent brought to an end 130 years of coal carriage by steamship.*

Malcolm Donnelly, South Shields

HUDSON SOUND 1950 2,577g Hudson Steamship Co. Ltd., London

The steamer **Hudson Sound** *only just qualifies as a coastal collier, although her owners had an impeccable pedigree as coastal shipowners. John Hudson and Co. began in business as coal distributors in 1842, in 1900 becoming part of the Samuel Williams group whose extensive interests along the Thames included Dagenham Dock. The company became shipowners out of necessity during the First World War when heavy losses from German U-boats and mines made it expensive to charter colliers. Much of the fleet, which became the Hudson Steamship Co. Ltd. in 1920, was lost during the Second World War and had to be replaced. The company bought colliers built during the war to standard designs and ordered five larger ships from the Ailsa Shipbuilding Co. Ltd. of Troon. Whilst*

the latter were being built, the major customers of the collier owners, the gas and electricity industries, were nationalised. The uncertainty surrounding this led to the **Hudson Sound** *being completed as suitable for trading to the Baltic or Mediterranean if the North East coal trade should begin to decline, and she carries an extensive set of derricks.*

When it came time to dispose of the **Hudson Sound** *after 17 years' service, she found owners in the USA. Crossing the Atlantic she worked in the West Indies, down to the River Plate and into the Pacific, under the names* **Rosella, Cathy** *and* **Vedalin**. *Not until 1973 was the steamer sold to breakers.*

Malcolm Donnelly, South Shields, 1st May 1965

EFFRA 1946 2,701g South Eastern Gas Board, London

Major industrial undertakings in their own right, British gas companies also had significant fleets of colliers. Shipowning began in 1902, initially to supply works which were sited up creeks to the east of London where traditional collier owners feared to tread. Expansion followed the outbreak of the First World War, when the colliers plying the East Coast coal routes were particularly vulnerable to U-boat attack, and the expensive investment in steamers was necessary to ensure regularity of coal supplies.

Named after a very minor tributary of the Thames, Effra was a post-Second World War ship, built at Sunderland where S.P. Austin and Son Ltd. specialised in colliers, long before they moved into the SD 14 Liberty replacements. Original owners were the South Metropolitan Gas Company which had an enormous gas works at East Greenwich.

Incidentally, if it can be cleaned up in time, this currently-derelict ground will serve as the Millennium Exhibition site. On 1st May 1949 the company was nationalised, but apart from a change of owner's title to South Eastern Gas Board, the fleet continued much as before. Effra was one of the Board's final colliers, not sold until 1967 when generation of gas from coal was ending. Despite her steam engines, flag-of-convenience operators then squeezed another seven years' service out of her hull, as Yannakis Fanis and Giulia, until she was broken up in Yugoslavia during 1974.

Note the crew man working in a precarious position atop the folded hatch covers.

Malcolm Donnelly, North Shields, 6th June 1962

JOHN ORWELL PHILLIPS   1955   3,391g   North Thames Gas Board, London

The Gas, Light and Coke Company was the doyen of gas producers, the first in the world when it obtained a charter in 1812, and growing to be the largest after commissioning its enormous Beckton works near Barking in 1870. Although obtaining powers to operate colliers as early as 1872, it did not exercise these until 1911 when it took delivery of the **Fulgens**. The name was derived from the company's motto Stet capitolium fulgens, a quotation from the Virgil's Aeneid which translates as 'Let the Capitol stand shining.'

The company came to supply gas to much of London north of the Thames, and on nationalisation of the gas industry in 1949 it transformed itself into the North Thames Gas Board. There was little external change, its funnel markings depicting red flames remaining, as did management by Stephenson Clarke which had begun with **Fulgens**. The imagination which had been used to name its earlier ships did desert it, however; and post-war colliers were given rather mundane names celebrating past engineers and managers, such as **John Orwell Phillips**. This large steamer was made redundant before its time by the industry's switch from coal gas to natural gas and in 1968 became the Panamanian **Agios Fanourios**. In April 1971 she was damaged in collision in the Fehmarn Belt, between Denmark and Germany, damage which - with her steam engines - meant that repair was uneconomic, and she was broken up in Norway.

Malcolm Donnelly, South Shields, 24th April 1965

SEAFORD 1947 1,108g
Stephenson Clarke Ltd., London

The collier companies were the last on the British coast to abandon steam. With coal continually pouring into their ships' holds, it was difficult to believe it would not continue to be readily and cheaply available to power their engines. Stephenson Clarke waited until after the war to try diesels, fitting a British Polar engine into their **Seaford**. *An advantage was immediately apparent: the more compact engines meant her deadweight and hence cargo capacity was significantly higher than her similar-sized steam contemporaries. Not surprisingly,* **Seaford** *outlasted many of the steamers in the fleet, and was not sold until 1971 when the moves from coal to oil for heating and from coal gas to natural gas saw the collier fleets being run down. A series of Greek owners squeezed some further life out of her, as* **Ciciliana, Georgios A, Alexis Athans** *and* **Panagia Kastrou**. *She had a rather ignominious fate: left untended she settled on the bottom at Alexandropoulis in December 1989 and was subsequently broken up.*

Harold Appleyard, Hartlepool

FINDON 1957 3,432g
Stephenson Clarke Ltd., London

Coasters are typically constrained in size by the ports they use and the consignments of cargo offering. In the coal trade, however, consignments kept getting bigger as gas works and later power stations were built larger and larger to benefit from economies of scale. With much of the coal being loaded on the Tyne and being delivered to utilities alongside the Thames or Medway, there were no restrictions on size, and so colliers grew with their cargoes. With her substantial bridge and accommodation aft, **Findon** *is really a small bulk carrier employed in a purely coastal trade.*

She came to Stephenson Clark in 1961 after running for four years as **Rondo** *for one of their rivals, Newcastle's Pelton Steamship Co. Ltd. On her sale by Stephenson Clarke in 1973 the quiet dignity of the Sussex village name of* **Findon** *was altered at a stroke to* **Indon**, *and subsequent names of* **San Shine** *and* **Triumph Ace** *were little better. During her first voyage under the latter name she stranded near Keelung on 27th September 1977 and was broken up in situ.*

Malcolm Donnelly, Dunston Staithes, River Tyne
17th September 1961

29

ARUNDEL   1956   3,422g   Stephenson Clarke Ltd., London

Despite the success of **Seaford** *her owners did not adopt oil engines for all their subsequent newbuildings. For their largest coastal colliers suitable oil engines were not available, and they retained steam propulsion. Nevertheless the engines had some of the sophistication of deep-sea machinery, with refinements such as oil firing and reheat.*

Arundel *had the distinction of being the very last steamer Stephenson Clarke had built, ending an unbroken line stretching back to the* **J.M. Strachan** *of 1865. The company could trace its origins far beyond that date, however; founders Ralph and Robert Clarke having bought shares in a sailing vessel in 1730. The son of the latter later moved to London to operate as a shipowner and coal factor, and married a Jane Stephenson to give the*

company's name. Stephenson Clarke remained independent until taken over by Powell Duffryn in 1928. Today, under different ownership, its ships with their silver-banded funnels can still be seen in UK ports although they seldom haul coal.

Arundel *was also the last Stephenson Clarke steamer in service, delivering her final cargo of coal from Harton Staithes on the Tyne to Dagenham in June 1972. She was then sold to Gino Gardella of Genoa who had a number of large ex-British colliers and gave her the name* **Brick Dodicesimo**. *After a period of lay up,* **Brick Dodicesimo** *was sold for breaking up in 1983.*

Malcolm Donnelly, South Shields, July 1969

NABULK   1955   1,307g
Maltese National Lines, Valletta

After the 1948 take-over of John Kelly Ltd. by Powell Duffryn Ltd. and William Cory and Son Ltd, the company was allowed to continue much as before, the only outward change being the adoption of names beginning Bally. The policy of ordering steamships was maintained right up until 1955, when the oil-fired **Ballylagan** *was delivered from Sunderland. Insufficient thought seems to have been given to this order, as* **Ballylagan** *was almost immediately lengthened. The surgery needed is apparent in this view of her in later life where the raised quarterdeck appears disproportionate in length to the well deck forward.*

When Kellys came to sell their last steamers in 1970, only the latest, **Ballylagan,** *could find a further owner. Initially owned in Larne as* **Dynabulker,** *in 1971 she was sold on and at a stroke (or more precisely, two strokes) renamed* **Nabulk.** *Extraordinary as it seems, the steamer was actually running on a liner service between Rotterdam and Malta when photographed. She had a few more years of life left, and as* **Thalassitra** *was broken up in Piraeus during 1980.*

Jim McFaul, Nieuwe Waterweg, 20th April 1973

BALLYRUSH   1962   1,575g
John Kelly Ltd., Belfast

Perhaps the problems with **Ballylagan** *persuaded Kelly's new owners that they should exert some influence over ship design. Subsequent ships like* **Ballyrush** *were diesel-powered and had a strong resemblance to those built for Stephenson Clarke, who were themselves owned by Powell Duffryn. The pole mainmast and the lightly streamlined but boxy superstructure aft were common features. Indeed, ships were occasionally exchanged between the two fleets, although the older ones tended to gravitate in the direction of the Belfast company.* **Ballyrush** *is probably fresh out of drydock in this view; the boot topping is almost gleaming, and her grey hull paint has been touched up. Kellys experimented with grey hulls for a while, but for the remainder of their existence they reverted to a more collier-like black.*

After 23 years with Kelly under one name, since her 1985 sale the motor collier has carried no fewer than seven: **Otterburn** *(for a Sunderland owner),* **Stina Star, Polly C, Polly Anna, Med Prince, Karim,** *and* **Haidar C.** *She was still trading in the Black Sea during August 1997.*

Stan Tedford, Belfast, 1969

31

FORTH   1943   869gt   William Sloan & Co., Glasgow

Forth is clearly a development of the **Mersey Coast** (page 19), a distinctive design which Coast Lines built in some numbers for its own fleet and those of its subsidiaries. The layout of the cargo gear, with a mixture of masts and kingposts, has been retained, but a bridge deck has been added and the rake to the bow is more restrained. The bridge amidships layout was well-liked by navigating officers, as it distanced their accommodation from the engines (and the engineers), and gave better visibility from the wheelhouse.

Built as **Southern Coast**, as with so many of Coast Lines' ships she was transferred amongst its subsidiaries on more than one occasion, usually adopting their traditional names and funnel colours. Having run between the Mersey and Belfast as **Colebrooke**

between 1955 and 1959, for three years she became the **Forth**, as seen here. Her owners William Sloan, a Glasgow concern dating from 1825, had just been acquired by Coast Lines. Sloan's surviving steamships were even older than **Forth**, which was drafted in as a replacement. After a further spell as **Southern Coast**, but now running to the Channel Islands, she was sold to Eastern Mediterranean owners in 1967. Under the names **Eleistria** and **Al Rubayia** she traded as far as India as a livestock carrier. She was laid up at Bombay early in 1983 and after over two years of inactivity sank at her moorings, subsequently being raised and broken up.

Malcolm Donnelly, North Shields, 5th June 1962

OLIVIAN COAST 1946 749gt Tyne-Tees Shipping Co. Ltd., Newcastle-upon-Tyne

Looking back from the late 1990s it is hard to appreciate the importance of coastal shipping in the 100 years up to the end of the First World War. One measure is the number and size of the fleets which were engaged in regular trading. Tyne-Tees Shipping Co. Ltd. were a major force in the business, running cargo and passenger services along the length of the East Coast and across the North Sea. Themselves the result of a merger of Newcastle and Middlesbrough-based companies in 1855, Tyne-Tees Shipping Co. Ltd. became part of the Coast Lines group during the Second World War. Appreciating the goodwill of the old-established company, the new owners changed neither name nor funnel colours, but did impose their own naming scheme. The motorship **Olivian Coast** *was one of the first newbuildings for Tyne-Tees under the new ownership, coming from the parent company's yard at Ardrossan and in design having a lot in common with ships like* **Mersey Coast** *and* **Forth**. *Her service for Tyne-Tees was remarkably constant, and only towards the end did she deviate from East Coast routes. In 1967 she was transferred to the British Channel Islands Shipping Co. Ltd. without change of name. In March 1968, however, she arrived at Bruges to be broken up. Tyne-Tees and Coast Lines survived only a few years longer, and in 1971 both were absorbed into P & O Short Sea Shipping Ltd., as the coastal shipping business continued to contract.*

Malcolm Donnelly, North Shields, 3rd June 1962

33

LOCHDUNVEGAN   1946   546g   David MacBrayne Ltd., Glasgow

The name David MacBrayne has a long connection with Clyde and West Highland steamer services, the founder being involved in the local passenger and cargo trades as far back as 1851. His name first appeared as a shipowner in his own right in 1879 and the MacBrayne connection continues with Caledonian-MacBrayne supplying many of the region's surviving car ferry services. David MacBrayne Ltd. was acquired jointly by the London, Midland and Scottish Railway and Coast Lines Ltd. in 1928, the railway share passing into state ownership in 1948.

MacBraynes' long traditions and a state share-holding makes it a little surprising that they would buy a Swedish vessel for their services, yet in 1950 the motorship **Orten** was acquired and renamed **Lochdunvegan**. British shipbuilding capacity was quite sufficient to

build all the ships needed, and looking overseas was regarded as almost treasonable. **Lochdunvegan**'s Swedish origins are apparent in treatment of her short superstructure, with much timber around the wheelhouse. She is also a flush decker and has a crane amidships: the latter feature was soon to become common, but amongst British owners was confined mainly to the General Steam Navigation's large fleet.

Although ice-strengthened, the motorship's career has seen her move further and further towards warmer climes. Following her Scottish service, she was sold to Greek owners in 1973 and became **Fanis** and in 1976 **Vassilis**. She was last reported under the Panama flag as **Maggy**.

Malcolm Donnelly, Greenock

LOCH CARRON   1951   683g   David MacBrayne Ltd., Glasgow

The motor vessel **Loch Carron** has impeccable credentials as a coastal and short-sea trader. She ran on general cargo services between Glasgow and Scottish islands such as Islay for over a quarter of a century, when many such trades had been lost to the container ship. Such little ships carried almost all the necessities of life for the island communities to which they traded, and the deck cargoes of the **Loch Carron** and of the **Lochdunvegan** opposite are to be noted. They include one of MacBraynes' buses and an early British Railways container.

Although shipping links were vital for the communities in the West of Scotland, the volume of cargo hardly justified sophisticated and expensive roll-on, roll-off ferry services, and it must be noted that the relaxed pace of life in the islands was much more suited to a somewhat leisurely conventional service. But the vehicle ferry did come, albeit belatedly, to Islay, and with it a deal of extra traffic not only on the island itself but on connecting roads on the mainland, bringing many additional but often uncounted costs.

Loch Carron was made redundant and was sold in 1977, subsequently trading under the names **Giorgis K**, **Eleni** and **Santa Maria**. Although still listed in Lloyd's Register as **Ranada** under the Honduras flag; lack of positive reports of her since visiting Piraeus in 1992 suggest she is laid up or has been broken up.

Malcolm Donnelly, Greenock, 2nd July 1965

35

SOMME 1950 451g Wm. H. Muller and Co. (London) Ltd., London

Today, many owners of small coasters build them with a low or retractable wheelhouse to allow them to penetrate the European inland waterway network to ports such as Duisburg-Ruhrort, Gainsborough or Brussels. But as the story of the 'flat-iron' colliers on page 24 relates, low air draught is nothing new, and even small, general cargo coasters have been built with this attribute for at least 70 years. An owner who specialised in such ships early was William Muller of Rotterdam, who in 1926 pioneered a service from Rotterdam to Paris with motor coasters which could pass beneath the Seine bridges The Parijs-vaart, *as these became known, later extended the services from Paris to the UK and the Iberian peninsula. For operations out of London, Muller found it convenient to have a local subsidiary and*

British-registered tonnage. Hence **Somme** *was built, very unusually for a Dutch owner, in a British yard - that of Henry Scarr Ltd. at Hessle on the Humber - and fitted with a British Polar diesel engine. She has low height superstructure, funnel and bridge, with no bridge deck, and her masts will be hinged.*

After a creditable 27 years with one name and one owner, things changed as one Greek or Panamanian owner after another bought her and applied their own ideas of appropriate names: **Doxa, Eliva, Asopi, St. Patrick** *and finally* **Antonello**. *She was broken up in Tunisia during 1989.*

Malcolm Donnelly, Greenock, 30th June 1965

BITTERN   1949   1,527g   British & Continental Steamship Co. Ltd., Liverpool

The steam-driven, engines-amidships short-sea trader was certified dead by many commentators in the 1930s but, as **Bittern** *shows, it refused to lie down. By 1949 the choice of steam reciprocating machinery was questionable for a ship like* **Bittern** *that would make regular, but relatively short passages, shuttling mainly from the Mersey to Antwerp and Rotterdam. Unlike a diesel engine, which could be shut down and restarted quickly, the steamer's boilers had to be kept alight - a wasteful operation when passages would seldom be long, and stops in ports frequent. The most likely explanation is that the owners were used to steam, and did not care to innovate at a time when trade was buoyant and there was little need for economy. The company certainly had more experience of steam than almost anyone else. Although its title dated only from 1922, it could trace its ancestry back to 1821 through the Cork Steamship Co. Ltd. and the St. George Steam Packet Co., whose funnel it inherited.*

Although her tonnage is small, **Bittern** *shares many features with a grown-up cargo liner, including four hatches, and a good outfit of cargo gear including a heavy-lift derrick at number 2 hold. Even her builders, Cammell, Laird & Co. Ltd. of Birkenhead, were more associated with ocean-going cargo ships than short-sea vessels.*

Bittern *left UK waters in 1966, but traded on in the Indian Ocean as* **Maldive Express** *until broken up on Gadani Beach in late 1975.*

Eddie Jackson, Eastham, River Mersey, January 1966

FRETHERNE　1950　351gt　H.K. Shaw, Gloucester

The captain-owner is a well-established figure in Dutch coastal shipping, where many shipowners began in business by borrowing the money to buy a ship and skippering it themselves. This was less common in the UK, at least since the heyday of coastal sail. Perhaps the best-known British protagonist was Captain Kenneth Shaw, who had started his seagoing career on his father's own auxiliary schooner in 1931, and went on to own a series of British and Dutch-built motor coasters. Fretherne was the third of these, bought in 1971 after spending over 20 years under the Dutch flag as Campen, Favoriet and Eagle 2. Registered in Gloucester – perhaps the last seagoing-vessel to carry the town's name on her stern – the motorship was named after a village near Captain Shaw's home at

Arlingham on the River Severn. Captain Shaw sold Fretherne in 1981 in favour of a slightly newer and larger coaster, the Zanzibar, and the Fretherne became the Jonsue for King's Lynn owner John Parsons, whose wife was presumably named Susan. Jonsue retired from coasting in 1986, becoming a stationary training ship at Fosdyke. In 1991 she sank at her moorings, and salvage work damaged her further, so she was sold for scrap. Captain Shaw himself retired in the same year at the age of 75, largely because even an operator of his experience found it uneconomic to run a small ship in the coastal trades.

Len Bath, Great Yarmouth, August 1977

RAKET 1952 328g N.V. 'Raket', Groningen

From early motor vessels like the **Confid** *(page 18) the design of the Dutch coaster evolved steadily, though without any significant innovations.* **Raket** *has a hull like the Dutch-built* **Fretherne**, *but her cargo gear is arranged rather differently. The single mast amidships allows a derrick to serve each hatch, but it is also hinged to permit passage under the low bridges which abound on Dutch inland waterways. The give-away is the vertical offset to the derricks, an arrangement which permits them to be stowed more easily when the mast is folded. To display her lights and fly the Dutch ensign,* **Raket** *also has a small mizzen mast with its own derrick for stores and for handling her boat.*

Raket *seems to have enjoyed a relatively quiet life. Her owners remained anonymous*

behind a single ship company: the N.V. in the title standing for 'Naamlooze Vennootschap', Dutch for limited company. And neither did the plain yellow funnel give any clues to ownership. In 1959 they moved responsibility for the day-to-day management of their ship from J.J. Onnes of Groningen to N.V. Scheepvaartbedrijf 'Gruno' of Amsterdam, but little else disturbed **Raket**'s *24 years under one name. In 1976 she was sold to the government of the Comoro Islands, a former French colony in the Indian Ocean. As* **Moinantsi** *she would have traded locally, but no recent movements have been reported for her and she has probably been laid up, perhaps following a breakdown of her original Dutch diesel engine.*

Paul Boot, Nieuwe Waterweg, 15th May 1976

HAWTHORN 1952 1,088g S. William Coe and Co. Ltd., Liverpool

Coal is virtually absent from Ireland, and all its industrial and domestic requirements have had to be imported, much to the benefit of Irish, English and Scottish collier owners. Railway locomotive coal was a particular need, and South Welsh steam coal was preferred. With Irish railways nationalised, it was natural that the state shipping company, Irish Shipping Ltd., would handle this trade. The company therefore ordered from Goole the **Irish Heather**, a neat little motorship to the traditional bridge amidships, raised quarter deck design. Alas, such planning did not foresee the early dieselisation of Irish railways, and other employment had to be found for the collier. After working the coal trade out of Goole as **Harglen**, in 1968 she passed to an old-established Liverpool owner, S. William

Coe and Co. Ltd. Coes renamed her **Hawthorn** and put her back into Irish Sea services, particular the coal and general cargo trade to the port of Coleraine. In 1973 she went back to Irish owners as **Howth Trader**, but her age meant she was now put under the Panama flag. Two years later she become the **Al Akber** and as such was last heard of in March 1985 at Karachi, a long way from the Irish Sea for which she was built. Panama deregistered **Al Akber** in 1988, and Lloyd's Register finally gave up hope of further information and deleted her late in 1991, assuming she had been broken up.

Roy Fenton, leaving Eastham Locks, Manchester Ship Canal, 8th April 1973

EMERALD   1952   1,382g   William Robertson (Shipowners) Ltd., Glasgow

Emerald *appears to be straining against a stiff breeze here, and this may be taken as symbolic of the determination of her company's founder to go against the wind and introduce powered vessels into a preserve of the sailing ship. In the 1870s the coal, stone and ore trades around the west of Scotland were still very much the province of schooners and ketches, but William Robertson showed that steamers could be made to pay in such work. Indeed, so successful was he that within two decades he had one of the largest fleets of steam coasters in the UK, all distinguished with names of precious stones or minerals. Another distinctive feature of the 'Gem Line' steamers was a white line neatly painted amidships below the bridge. After 1936 Robertsons slowly introduced motorships, and*

these developed into a raised quarter deck design that was very much the company's own, with a boxy superstructure topped by a squat, black funnel. The bridge had moved aft to join the rest of the accommodation but, as can be seen on the **Emerald,** *the white line moved aft with it.*

The third Robertson ship to carry the name, **Emerald** *was sold in 1975, finding the Mediterranean owners who took so many old British motorships. She first became the Greek* **Ioannis D,** *then the Lebanese* **Hanadi** *and finally* **Rania.** *Breakers at Perama in Greece brought her career to an end in 1986.*

Paul Boot, Nieuwe Waterweg, 30th May 1974

DIMITRIOS G   1952   1,812g   Michael Gigilinis, Thessalonika

Comben Longstaff (no comma, Comben was Mr. Longstaff's middle name) began building up his coastal shipping business in 1933, and established himself in the East Coast coal trade. During the war he built up a remarkably motley fleet, taking whatever steamers he could buy but making a reasonable profit from them. Post-war he began building ships, and as his previous experience with motorships was unfavourable, he chose steam engines. In the early 1950s he ordered two ships from Aberdeen, the steamer **Cardiganbrook** and the externally almost identical **Cardiffbrook** which had a diesel engine. Indeed, the former could be told from the latter, which is seen here in later life, only by stokehold vents just forward of the funnel.

It is tempting to assume there was a comparison going on, but during his researches the author of a recent history of the fleet failed to find any evidence of this in company minutes. Indeed, the three-cylinder Doxford engine fitted to **Cardiffbrook** was more suitable for a trawler (for which it had been built) and being slow and difficult to manoeuvre did not suit a coaster. If it was a trial, the company did not wait for the results but ordered another steamer almost immediately.

Cardiffbrook and her near-sister both lasted 17 years in the company's ownership, but the motorship has had a longer subsequent career. Seen here with her first Greek owner, she became the **Marietta** in 1972 and lasted until 1983. The former **Cardiganbrook** had been broken up in 1970.

J. Wiltshire, Avonmouth, 4th June 1971

BRIGHT SKY   1955   1,308g   Catapola Shipping Co. Ltd., Piraeus

*Although Coast Lines were primarily interested in regular liner services, they also had companies which were involved in home-trade tramping. Of these, Queenship Navigation Ltd. of London was closely associated with Coast Lines' Channel Islands operations. The company's naming scheme reflected that of the original company in this trade, the London and Channel Islands Steamship Co. Ltd., and its most important trade was coal from Goole or Blyth to the Channel Islands or south west ports. In the mid-1960s, however, Coast Lines decided to divest themselves of their tramps; in truth they had enough problems in attempting to adapt to the unit load and roll-on, roll-off revolutions which were affecting the group's traditional trades. In 1965 **Sandringham Queen** and several others were sold to*

*companies owned by Watts Watts and Co. Ltd., a deep-sea tramping concern who placed their management with Comben Longstaff & Co. Ltd. **Sandringham Queen** retained her name until sold in 1972 when she hoisted the rather anaemic-looking Cyprus flag and became the **Bright Sky**. A change of ownership in 1976 saw her name become **Greek Sky**, and as this the former queen was broken up in Italy early in 1983.*

*The hull design of **Bright Sky** was a very common one for British post-war motor coasters, as witness **Emerald**, **Corkbrook**, and **Derwent Fisher**. It resulted from taking a standard raised quarter deck hull and moving the bridge aft to join the rest of the superstructure.*

Roy Fenton, Eastham, River Mersey, 7th April 1973

LAIRDS LOCH   1944   1,736g   Burns and Laird Lines Ltd., Glasgow

The first use of steamships was on short sea routes such as those between Ireland and England and Scotland where their speed and regularity justified the high cost compared with sailing craft. Hence, companies specialising in these routes are often amongst the oldest steam shipping companies. Burns and Laird Lines Ltd. was an amalgamation in 1922 of two venerable companies, G. and J. Burns which was founded in 1824, and Laird Line which could trace its formation back to 1814. The amalgamation resulted from the acquisition by Coast Lines Ltd. of the two companies which operated competing services from the Clyde to Northern Ireland. Burns used names of animals and birds, whilst Laird Line favoured plants, but both flora and fauna were swept away in an enthusiasm for giving all ships names commencing Laird.

*The twin-screw motor vessel **Lairds Loch** was an unusual example of an owner being allowed to complete a ship to their own design during wartime, which is rather odd as the service she was intended for - Glasgow to Londonderry - was suspended during hostilities. She was finished as a pure cargo ship, her planned passenger accommodation being added later.*

*After sale by Burns and Laird in 1969, **Lairds Loch** returned to Ardrossan for adaptation for use in the Red Sea. As **Hey Daroma** the Israeli-owned vessel was wrecked in the Gulf of Aqaba during September 1970 whilst on her regular service from Eilat to Sharm-el-Sheikh.*

Malcolm Donnelly, Greenock

MALDIVE IMPORTER   1956   1,372g   Maldives Shipping Ltd., Maldive Islands

Seen here far from her original haunts is a late example of a type of ship now extinct in British waters, the short-sea cargo passenger ship. As **Kirkham Abbey** *she was built to run from Goole to Copenhagen. For this she had accommodation for 12 first class passengers in her ample superstructure, and for the carriage of Denmark's exports was fitted with refrigerating machinery; essential for butter and bacon, less so for lager and Lego. Original owners were Associated Humber Lines, but in 1965 the Goole to Copenhagen service was sold to Ellerman's Wilson Line Ltd. of Hull, and with it the* **Kirkham Abbey** *and her sister* **Byland Abbey***. For a period there was no change, but in 1967* **Kirkham Abbey** *was switched to her new owner's service from London to Copenhagen and Aarhus. Here there*

was little point in perpetuating the attractive names of Yorkshire monastic foundations, and in 1968 the Ellerman Wilson name **Ariosto** *was bestowed on the motorship.*

Only two years later, in 1970, the Hull company disposed of the ship, the trend to containerisation for cargo and big ferries for passengers making the cargo passenger ship obsolete. At the time companies in the Maldive Islands avidly bought surplus British tonnage - there was plenty available - and she became **Maldive Importer***, her sister becoming, with no great effort of imagination,* **Maldive Exporter***. Both were broken up at Gadani Beach, Pakistan; the* **Maldive Importer** *arriving there in August 1983.*

Nigel Jones, Singapore, 10th February 1983

URANIA   1955   1,839g   Astrosuerte Corporation, Monrovia (J.P. Hadoulis Ltd., London)

The steamer **Urania** *shows the ultimate manifestation of the engines-amidships short-sea trader, with cargo gear against the superstructure to give maximum deck space and high-set derricks to clear a timber cargo. In layout, she is very similar to the* **Tyne** *on page 8, a ship built 35 years earlier. She was an anachronism in 1955 and can hardly be thought of as a tribute to either her Scottish builders or her original owners. The latter was none other than Fred Olsen of Oslo - not since noted for conservatism - for whom she was completed as* **Bruin**. *Perhaps it is surprising that* **Bruin** *remained in their fleet as long as she did: not sold until 1968 to become* **Alexandra Maris**. *The name she is pictured under,* **Urania**, *was adopted in 1969.*

With her forecastle and bridge bulwarks picked out in white, **Urania** *is in smart condition, despite being under the Liberian flag. Her ultimate owners were members of the London-Greek shipowning fraternity who traditionally had pride in their vessels, even if old. A nice touch is that her main topmast and the upper parts of the aft kingposts are painted black, reflecting the likelihood of their being soot-blackened by the exhaust from a steamer.*
Further sales in 1975 saw her become **Urania III** *and quickly* **Stardust**. *Damaged by stranding in January 1976, her obsolete machinery meant she did not warrant repair and* **Stardust** *was broken up.*

Malcolm Donnelly, South Shields, 24th July 1969

HERON 1957 943g General Steam Navigation Co. Ltd., London

The owners of **Heron** *claimed to be the world's first company to own sea-going steamers, the Clyde Shipping Company being older but operating only river craft in its earliest days. The General Steam Navigation Company was granted its charter in 1824, and set out with the bold objectives of trading by steam to Russia, India, North and South America, the Iberian peninsula and - more realistically - France and Holland. In the event those wishing to navigate by steam to the further flung of these destinations had to wait patiently whilst the steamship evolved, and despite its name the company contented itself with services to Spain and Portugal and later to the Mediterranean. However, the company exploited its pioneering status to spin a tight web of European services which continued to employ a*

significant fleet right up to the 1950s. But like Coast Lines, a similarly once-great company, General Steam adapted itself poorly to the roll-on, roll-off and unit load revolutions, and in the early 1970s it all but disappeared.

Basically a small cargo liner, **Heron** *was a typical example of General Steam's larger short-sea traders, with generous crew accommodation and ample cargo gear. She lasted almost until the end of General Steam, being sold in 1969. Following yearly name changes - first* **Thelma P**, *then* **Anastasia**, *and finally* **Express 1** *- she and her unfortunate crew disappeared in the Mediterranean during December 1973 when carrying magnesite from Piraeus to Leghorn.* Malcolm Donnelly, North Shields, 1963

THE LADY GWENDOLEN 1953 1,166g A. Guinness, Son and Co. (Dublin) Ltd., Dublin

The history of shipping Guinness from Dublin to the UK is a long one, and each successive generation of ship has made its contribution to the development of the trade. In 1913 a steam collier was bought and, although torpedoed only four years later, showed the brewery the desirability of having its own ships. Three younger colliers were then bought, some of which had cooling plant installed to keep the casks of stout in good condition. In 1931 came the first ship specially built for the trade, the steamer **Guinness** (front cover). In 1952 and 1953 the remaining colliers were replaced by two new motorships: **The Lady Gwendolen** and **The Lady Grania**. To all outward appearances these were conventional dry cargo coasters, but in their holds they carried the Guinness in 500-gallon tanks rather than casks. This contributed to the economics of the operation, but it is debatable whether it added to the taste of the stout. In 1962 **The Lady Patricia** arrived to make the **Guinness** redundant, and was herself later converted into a bulk beer tanker. In 1976 the building of the tanker **Miranda Guinness** made **The Lady Gwendolen** redundant and she became the Piraeus-owned **Paros**. On 10th November 1979 she was run down and sunk whilst at anchor in Ravenna Roads. Sadly, the carriage of Guinness in brewery-owned ships has not survived. The two tankers were scrapped in the 1990s, the beer now being carried in tanks on container ships.

Eddie Jackson, Eastham, River Mersey, August 1973

48

LADY ROSLIN 1958 698g Nobel's Explosives Co. Ltd., Stevenston

This was another Lady which carried a product that needed careful handling. The orange bulwarks of **Lady Roslin** *were part of her owner's contemporary livery, but they might also have served as a warning that she was not to be trifled with. She habitually carried explosives from Ayrshire, where Swedish armaments manufacturer Alfred Nobel established his British factory. His company was one of the founding partners of ICI.*

It was not a good idea to carry large quantities of explosives, and **Lady Roslin's** *appearance reflects this, with relatively short holds and a long poop deck. Such a specialised ship might have found it difficult to find further purchasers once Nobels had finished with her, but this was not the case. In 1982 she became the* **Aragonite**, *and had*

quite an adventure. The Falklands War saw the regular ship serving St. Helena requisitioned as a minesweeper support ship. To offer a temporary replacement **Aragonite** *was converted to carry 12 passengers - presumably in the generous crew accommodation already provided. The voyage down to the South Atlantic in such a small ship is better imagined than experienced.*

Having proved she was made of stout stuff, the little coaster found further owners as **Silver Sea** *and* **My Dream**. *Although still listed in Lloyd's Register, there have been no reports of movements since 1993, and it must be assumed that* **My Dream** *is slumbering quietly in some backwater, recalling her past exploits.* Stan Tedford, Gothenborg, 1978

49

CENTURY   1956   780g   F.T. Everard & Sons Ltd., London

Eccentricity characterises Everard's naming scheme. The name has never been used, but **Centricity** *certainly has. Although many of its names can be found if the dictionary is comprehensive enough, some of the -ity names were certainly invented to suit the type of ship – such as* **Tankity** *(see page 53) – or the occasion – such as* **Century**. *The latter name was bestowed upon what was reputed to have been the one hundredth ship built for the owners. Although the number of vessels passing through their hands was over 200 by this time, it is hard to find half this number which were actually built for Everards, even when their sailing barges and tugs are counted.*

Century *was built at Goole, and was distinguishable from her near-sisters by the kingpost sited immediately abaft of the bridge: most motor coasters of this period made do with the*

two masts and derricks which had sufficed for the two-hatch steam coaster. Judging by the white stains on her hull, **Century** *had been carrying china clay from a Cornish port to Runcorn, from where she was outward bound when photographed. This trade dated from 1777 when the Trent and Mersey Canal was built. For many years the coasters arriving at Runcorn would have unloaded the clay directly into narrow boats for delivery to the Potteries.*

Century *was sold in 1975 and renamed* **Tempesta** *under the Cyprus flag, but was deleted from Lloyds's Register in 1987 because current information about her existence was lacking.*

Roy Fenton, River Mersey, 6th September 1975

SANGUITY   1956   1,577g   F.T. Everard & Sons Ltd., London

The classic British coaster design originated in the 1880s, with its bridge positioned at the break of the raised quarterdeck and a well between it and the forecastle. The welldeck was a result of an aberration in the rules, but the quarterdeck was a sound design feature which helped move the centre of gravity aft so that the ship trimmed evenly when loaded. Certainly the design was well proven over time, and three quarters of a century later it was perpetuated in many British motorships.

Sanguity was one of Everard's celebrated 'S' class, ten of which were completed at intervals over the period 1949 to 1958. Built at Goole or (as was **Sanguity***) Grangemouth, all had diesel machinery made well inland at Newbury, the engine builder being a subsidiary of the*

owners. Their yellow hulls signified their suitability for grain cargoes but inevitably led to them being dubbed 'yellow perils'. With their balanced profile and attractive wooden wheelhouses they became a well-loved part of the coasting scene, lasting well into the 1970s. For once looks matched performance, and the 'S' class proved themselves reliable and versatile ships which could carry a wide variety of coastal cargoes. And with a gross tonnage just below 1,600 they escaped the expense of having to carry a radio officer. Sold in 1978, **Sanguity** *was renamed* **Ramona** *and, partly due to a lengthy lay-up at Oslo, survived until broken up at Bruges at the end of 1994.*

Paul Boot, Nieuwe Waterweg, 30th May 1974

KATERINA V   1958   2,739g   Ortansia Shipping Co. S.A. (Varnima Corporation), Piraeus

*The basic hull shape which Everards used for dry cargo vessels was adapted for their tankers with the addition of a trunk: compare the present ship with **Sanguity**. Starting with **Anteriority** in 1954, through the **Assurity** of 1956 to the **Grit** of 1958, each new tanker represented an advance in size, built to carry just that extra drop of cargo and so earn more. However, they met Everard's definition of a coaster as a vessel which could get into Goole. All three tankers were time-chartered to Esso Petroleum for ten years, but when these contracts ended Everards could find little work for them, and they had the additional problem of serious corrosion in tanks which had never received a protective coating. All*
*were sold, and **Grit** became **Eleni** and in 1973 **Katerina V**, as seen here. She traded under this name for ten years during which time she visited some of her old haunts, as seen here in the Manchester Ship Canal where the verdant fields of South Lancashire end abruptly at the industrial environs of Manchester. It is pleasing to note that she kept the hardwood cladding of her wheelhouse and bridge wings. In 1985 she became the **Alnour** but was broken up in Greece a year later. Despite the corrosion she had survived for 18 years after Everard ownership.*

John Slavin, Warburton, Manchester Ship Canal, July 1974

TANKITY   1945   145g   F.T. Everard & Sons Ltd., London

Military oil barges, or MOBs, sounded a good idea at the time the Normandy landings were being planned. They were designed to carry liquid products such as diesel and motor spirit to forward positions to supply military units. So that they could be used in distant theatres of war their hulls were built in three pieces which could be carried by heavy-lift ships, and several MOBs made their way out to Malta this way. But tardiness in placing the orders - or lack of shipbuilding capacity - meant few were ready until the war was almost ended, and they tended to serve in less glorious roles as water lighters at Cuxhaven and on the Rhine. Completed on the Tyne in 1945, just 12 years later **MOB 7** *was sold by the Admiralty to Pounds, the Portsmouth company who purported to be shipbreakers, but who sold her on*

to Everards. She joined four other MOBs in the fleet, which were mainly used to bunker ships and supply shore establishments such as power stations. Under the splendid name **Tankity** *she worked for ten years, mostly on Merseyside where she is seen here with Clarence Dock Power Station in the background. Note her rather home-made appearance and her minimal freeboard.* **Tankity** *gained the reputation of being one of the few ships using the Manchester Ship Canal which could actually turn round anywhere on the waterway. In 1967* **Tankity** *was sold to real shipbreakers and demolished at Dalmuir.*

World Ship Photo Library, Birkenhead

POLARIS 1956 1,518g Finska Ångfartygs Ab, Helsinki

Finska Ångfartygs Ab - EFFOA or the Finland Steamship Company to its friends - was formed in 1883, principally to export Finnish butter to the UK, although services to the Mediterranean and along the Finnish coast were soon added. Suffering heavy losses through both world wars, the company also faced the problem of having to give many of its ships as reparations to the USSR because Finland had the effrontery to defend itself against its big neighbour. However, EFFOA fought back, and through newbuildings and purchases its fleet reached its greatest extent in the 1950s. Like many of its new ships, the motor vessel **Polaris** *and her sister* **Astrea** *came from a Dutch yard. Their rather rakish lines were partly as a result of the icebreaker bows which were essential for any serious navigation in*

Finnish waters during winter. The design was a transitional one, intermediate between the rather conservative three island, engines amidships types and the engines-aft design with its multitude of kingposts which characterised EFFOA's newbuilding in the 1960s. Common to **Polaris** *and most of these were bridge plating which is extended to wrap around the winch platforms in order to offer a modicum of protection to the operator in the Arctic winter. In 1973* **Polaris** *was sold to Italian owners who put her under the Panama flag as* **Speedmarit**, *only to sell her to Lebanese owners under whose care she survived as* **Jamil** *until 1995.*

Paul Boot, Eastham, River Mersey, 16th July 1972

KLJAFOSS 1957 500g Eimskipafélag Reykjavikur H/F, Reykjavik

Coasters on regular liner services typically need more extensive cargo gear than their brethren in the tramp trades. The regular trader often handled smaller parcels of general cargo, and typically called at several ports during a single voyage. Hence the **Kljafoss** *has six derricks where two would suit a similar-sized contemporary designed for bulk cargo carrying. Although not apparent in the photograph,* **Kljafoss** *had a shelter deck, an extra deck worked into her hull which facilitated stowing parcels of cargo which might be taken on or discharged at intermediate ports on her voyage.*

She was built in Denmark as **Askja***, a name only marginally easier to get an English tongue round than* **Kljafoss***, which she became in 1976. This change did not signify new*

ownership, only a standardisation on names of waterfalls by her owners who were widely known as the Iceland Steamship Co. for reasons apparent to any non-Icelander trying to pronounce its native title.

It is somewhat ironic that an ice-strengthened ship should eventually find buyers at the eastern end of the Mediterranean. It was probably her extra deck that appealed to the Lebanese who bought **Kljafoss** *in 1980 and renamed her* **Khalil II***. She subsequently became a livestock carrier, a conversion for which her shelter deck well suited her. Names easy on the ear have never been part of her career, and as the* **Tweit II** *she still conveys her noisy and probably smelly cargoes around the Levant.* Nigel Bowker, Mersey, 1st May 1977

55

CON ZELO 1957 400g Jeppeson Heaton Ltd., London

Apart from one small detail, **Con Zelo** *could pass for the classic Dutch coaster of post-war years. She has masts tidily stepped on the break of forecastle and poop to allow stowage of a timber deck cargo. Each mast has the 'acorn' which is almost a trade mark of Dutch builders. Her derricks have gone, however, a reflection of almost universal shoreside craneage being provided at her typical berths. With no need of the ship's own cargo gear, derricks were sent ashore to decrease the maintenance required and to reduce top hamper. Purists would argue that this spoilt the lines of a ship, although some vessels suffered much more than* **Con Zelo***, with their masts being reduced to mere poles to carry navigation lights. The black-painted tabernacles in which the* **Con Zelo's** *masts were set to allow them*

to be hinged can be clearly seen.

The detail that makes **Con Zelo** *atypical is that, despite carrying a Dutch name, she spent most of her career with a British owner, who bought her in 1962. Only in 1990 did she pass out of British registry, being renamed* **Femi** *under the flag of St. Vincent and the Grenadines. As so often, this was a flag of convenience, and her real owner was German. The good fortune that kept the coaster out of serious trouble finally deserted her, and in 1993* **Femi** *was reported laid up under arrest at Lipari in Italy, doubtless awaiting an appointment with the breakers.*

Les Hodder, River Trent, 26th August 1981

ANNE HERFURTH 1961 500g Herfurth Scheepvaart & Transportbedrijf N.V., Rotterdam

The Dutch coaster enjoyed a period of unprecedented prosperity in the late 1940s and 1950s. Their grey hulls could be seen in trades throughout Europe and often beyond, exploiting the economies of the diesel engine. Further savings often came from employing the captain-owner's family as part of the crew and having captain or mate double up as engineer. Yet the prosperity engendered some complacency, with the result that coaster design in Holland tended to ossify. **Anne Herfurth** looks quite a picture here, although her paintwork needs touching up. Her houseflag is flying bravely as she enters her home port of Rotterdam, and she still has her full complement of cargo gear. But in reality she was something of an anachronism, being built in 1961 to a design that had been worked out in all of its details 20 years earlier. She even has the wooden wheelhouse which delights enthusiasts but was a costly indulgence at 1960s prices.

A year after this photograph was taken **Anne Herfurth** was sold to owners who put her under the Panama flag as **Asuncion**. The pride with which a Dutch coaster was typically maintained was replaced with an indifference and even malevolence to the little ship. On 9th September 1980, whilst on a voyage from Yugoslavia to Libya, the crew abandoned her, complaining that she had started taking on water. The master and engineer were subsequently arrested on suspicion of scuttling the vessel.

Paul Boot, Nieuwe Waterweg, 11th May 1973

HELGA HAUSCHILDT 1957 425g Heinrich Hauschildt, Hamburg

No review of coasters would be complete without coverage of the German vessels which, eclipsing even the Dutch, came to dominate short-sea trades in the 1980s and 1990s. This achievement is the more remarkable when the state of the Handelsmarine in May 1945 is considered, with most of the ships still afloat bomb damaged, and those which could be repaired mainly taken by the victorious Allies. Starting modestly with surviving old tonnage, gradually adding second-hand Dutch ships, and then developing its own coaster-building industry, Germany built up a fleet which is now probably three times larger than that of its nearest competitors, the Dutch. Behind this success has been much hard work and solid investment, as well as considerable bending of the rules to ensure favourable

tonnage measurements, registration status and subsidies.

This example was built as **Christa II** *at a slightly obscure yard at Neuenfelde on the Elbe - a river which has been the home and birthplace of many such coasters. The name* **Helga Hauschildt** *was carried from 1960: note the colourful hull which is a welcome feature introduced to the coastal scene by German and Scandinavian owners. In 1966 she became* **Sondith** *and since 1983 has sailed under the Ecuadorian flag as* **Paola**. *This reflects genuine ownership in South America; one of the devices used by German coaster owners to cut costs has been to run their ships under third world flags but to retain local registration.*

Malcolm Donnelly, North Shields, 6th June 1962

MARIE TH 1961 400g G.B. Theusen Partrederi, Faaborg

The rise of the Dutch coaster in the years following the Second World War was paralleled by a mushrooming of the fleet owned in Denmark. Whilst not decrying the seagoing enterprise of the Danes - which dates back at least to Viking times - this growth owed a lot to fiscal measures. Danes who invested in shipping obtained substantial tax concessions, and to encourage small investors to do this many partrederi *- part ownership companies - were set up. This was often greatly to the benefit of established ship management companies, who found their business considerably expanded. One such was A.E. Sorensen of Svendborg who managed the trim little motor coaster* **Marie Th** *for a Faaborg* partrederi. *Her credentials as a representative of Danish coasters are not completely*

satisfactory, however. Although she was constructed for Danes as **Louis S**, *her builders were at Husum in Germany and were clearly influenced by Dutch coaster design. Perhaps because the expansion of the Danish fleet was not founded on solid commercial reasoning, it faltered in the 1980s and the number of Danish coasters has since declined. However,* **Marie Th**, *as she became in 1974, sailed on under Danish ownership as* **Rita L** *after 1984 and at the time of writing is still actively trading as* **Lake Pejo**. *She was photographed entering the Manchester Ship Canal an unusually long time after high water, hence the acreage of sand and mud in the background.*

Roy Fenton, Eastham, River Mersey, 11th October 1975

CORKBROOK 1964 1,594g Comben Longstaff & Co. Ltd., London

Corkbrook *was a standard design by her Tyneside builders, Clelands Shipbuilding Co. Ltd. They called it XL 2400, the figure referring to the deadweight of the prototype. Although following the familiar raised quarter deck design, it was unusual in having so much open deck space aft of the superstructure. Over the subsequent 30 years designers have done their utmost to maximise the area of a coaster's hatches in order to stow as many containers as possible on a given hull length and today such wasted areas would be unthinkable. Comben Longstaff took four like* **Corkbrook,** *plus the prototype* **Cornishbrook** *which did not have the open area aft, nor did it have the winch platform by the mainmast apparent in* **Corkbrook**. *This was an improvement to the prototype which*

meant the steel hatch covers could be rolled right back to give the maximum hatch opening. Everards also bought three XL 2400s.

The **Corkbrook** *and her sisters traded widely, suggesting that the term coaster is inadequate for craft which could happily serve Canada, the White Sea and Mediterranean ports. It is likely that uncertainties in the Mediterranean trade led Comben Longstaff to sell all their ships of the type in 1976, for they were far from worn out.* **Corkbrook** *then had a series of Greek owners, who called her* **Neapolis II, Lakonikos** *and* **Ygia.** *Since 1996 she has been named* **Durbala** *under the Belize flag, and was still actively trading in August 1997.*

Paul Boot, Eastham, River Mersey, 1st July 1972

KINNAIRD HEAD 1963 1,985g A.F. Henry & McGregor Ltd., Leith

*It is difficult to know whether to classify **Kinnaird Head** as a large coaster or a small collier. Her Leith-based owners certainly maintained an involvement in the coal trade along the east coasts of Scotland and England. And her brown superstructure was a mark of a coal trade ship: presumably it did not show the dirt. But the ample outfit of derricks would not be needed for a collier, which was invariably loaded and discharged by highly efficient shoreside gear. Her Scottish owners undoubtedly hedged their bets, building a vessel which could work as a collier but could move to other bulk trades when the need arose. And the need for alternative employment for colliers certainly did arise through the late 1960s and 1970s as, for economic and political reasons, coal lost its place to oil as the UK's major*

source of power. Her sailing from the Manchester Ship Canal in ballast confirms she was not in the coal trade at the time of the photograph.

Kinnaird Head *changed hands in 1972, moving from Leith to Guernsey ownership. Her Channel Islands' owners also had a history of shipping coal, largely to Guernsey for heating its greenhouses. The delightfully-named Onesimus Dorey (Shipowners) Ltd. gave her one of his traditional Guernsey names,* **Perelle**. *In 1977 she moved to owners on another island, Sardinia. Registered in Cagliari she became* **Francesca Seconda**. *In 1985, and at no great age, she was sold for demolition to breakers at Porto Nogaro.*

Paul Boot, Eastham, River Mersey, 4th February 1972

BEN VEG   1965   346g   Ramsey Steamship Co. Ltd., Ramsey

The Ramsey Steamship Company was formed in 1914 to operate coasters suitable for using the small Manx and other ports around the Irish Sea, and has proved constant to this aim, still trading with a fleet of three small motorships in 1997. Despite having owned over two dozen ships, only four have been built for the company. Ben Veg was one of these, built by Clelands Shipbuilding Co. Ltd., and in recognition of her status she took the name of the company's first steamer, which means 'little woman' in Manx. The name was most appropriate: with her cargo gear and full height forecastle and poop, she is a fine 1960s interpretation of the classic little Irish Sea coaster design.

After only 13 years the Ben Veg was sold after sustaining severe damage and on being repaired went out to the West Indies to be renamed simply Benn. Her fate sadly reflects that of many European coasters which, through want of money or repairing skills, were allowed to rust away or met an even worse fate. In September 1989 she was in Venezuela needing repairs, and was towed to Trinidad for these to be carried out. During welding work at Port of Spain she caught fire, but although damage was minor, it was then necessary to tow her to Castries in January 1991 for further work. During heavy weather the towline broke, and the unmanned Benn is presumed to have sunk.

Paul Boot, Eastham, River Mersey, 10th May 1972

DERWENT FISHER   1966   1,096g   James Fisher & Sons Ltd., Barrow-in-Furness

Derwent Fisher *is the most recently-built coaster in this book, but has a number of features which can be considered classic. The hatch tops are level to facilitate carrying containers and to allow the use of mechanical hatch covers, part of the gear for which can be seen at the after end of the well. But despite this, her raised quarter deck hull has a satisfying degree of sheer. The gentle curve to the bridge front, her rounded funnel casing, and sloping stanchions to the superstructure: all these contribute to a design whose visual aspects have been well considered. She is a tribute to her builders, who happen to be Dutch, and to her owners, who can claim to be one of the oldest British coastal shipowners, tracing their involvement back to the days of wooden schooners.*

As a revenue earner, **Derwent Fisher** *has also succeeded, despite her derricks being too short for the holds they are meant to serve. Fishers kept her until 1979, when she became* **Parham** *for a small owner in Ipswich. She soon left the British flag for that of Honduras; cheaper and much less fussy about standards of crewing and maintenance. After 1984 came a succession of names, some attractive, some semi-literate:* **Sofia**, **Saint Anthonys**, **Golduen Bird**, **Mariya**, **Swene**, *and finally* **Baris B**. *Under the last of these she is owned in Turkey but registered in Malta, and still trades in the Black Sea.*

Nigel Bowker, Eastham, River Mersey, 30th July 1975

ROE DEER 1962 1,482g Tyne-Tees Steam Shipping Co. Ltd., Newcastle-upon-Tyne (P & O Ferries)

*The inclusion of this container ship amongst such august company may cause the odd eyebrow to be raised. However, **Roe Deer** was one of the first vessels built for what was soon to become a revolution in cargo carrying. Despite her innovative role, she differed little in appearance, save the omission of cargo handling gear, from the generation of conventional coasters which she followed. Her design incorporated many traditional features. The strong sheer line of the hull supported a finely-flared forecastle, plus a well-proportioned superstructure and cambered decks. Such features were soon to be abandoned, so **Roe Deer** is presented as a final manifestation of the classic coaster. Built at Ardrossan as **Buffalo** for Link Line, the pioneering unit load subsidiary of Coast*

*Lines, she entered service between Liverpool and Belfast with her sister **Bison**. In 1972 she was transferred within the parent P & O group, taking the plain orange funnel of North Sea Ferries Ltd. as **Norbrae**. A further change of name to **Roe Deer** came in 1974 when she adopted the colourful livery seen here for a Tilbury to Rotterdam service. This identity lasted only two years before she was sold to inaugurate a container service between Halifax and St. John's, Newfoundland as the appropriately, if unimaginatively, named **Newfoundland Container**. Subsequent changes saw her become **Caribbean Victory**, **Lefkimmi**, **St. Georg** and **Container Express**. She was deleted from the Belize registry in 1993 after being abandoned by her owners.* Paul Boot, Nieuwe Waterweg, 3rd May 1975